Global Haiku

Twenty-five Poets
World-wide

editors:
George Swede
Randy Brooks

IRON PRESS

mosaic press

First published jointly in 2000
by IRON Press (UK) and Mosaic Press (North America)

Printed by
AGMV

Typesetting by Kitty Fitzgerald in Garamond 12pt
Book design by Kitty Fitzgerald & Michael Adam
Cover design by Sarah Gibson & Peter Mortimer

ISBN 0-906-228-75-1

IRON Press
5, Marden Terrace
Cullercoats
North Shields
Northumberland, NE30 4PD
England
Tel/fax: (0191) 253 1901
Email: seaboy@freenetname.co.uk

IRON Press books are represented by
Signature Book Representation
Sun House
2 Little Peter St
Knott Mill
Manchester
M15 4PS
Tel: (0161) 8348767
Fax: (0161) 834 8656
Email signature@dircon.co.uk

CONTENTS

FOREWORD

Makoto Ueda

English poetry enriched itself considerably by assimilating the Italian *sonetto*. There would not have been the sonnets of Shakespeare or Milton or Wordsworth, or *The House of Life* or *Leda and the Swan* if the fourteen line form had not become part of the English literary tradition. Today however, we do not often think of early sixteenth century poets who contributed to the process through which the sonetto became the sonnet. To be sure, we pay some respect to Sir Thomas Wyatt and Henry Howard, Earl of Surrey as the two pioneers who first experimented with the foreign verse form. Yet there must have been a number of other contemporary poets who explored the poetic potential of the imported form in various ways, until some basic rules were established toward the end of the century. It was after decades of such experimentation that Spenser and Shakespeare came out to produce their beautiful lyrics in fourteen lines.

Some four hundred years later, English poetry is in the process of assimilating the Japanese *haiku*. The assimulation of the seventeen syllable form has been more problematic, because there lies a greater linguistic and cultural distance between Japanese and English verse. While those who tried to write sonetto in English could adopt the original stanzaic and rhyming scheme with only minor modifications, English poets who want to compose haiku have to devise their own form since the traditional Japanese poem uses no such scheme, not even lineation, to distinguish itself from prose. Whereas the Italian sonetto had a firm sense of closure, the Japanese haiku prefers an open ending, which runs counter to the traditional art of verse writing in English. Sonneteers in Elizabethan English had no great problem importing the subject of courtly love from Italy, but philosophical implications of the Japanese haiku, tinged with Zen Buddhism and a Taostic attitude towards nature, seem alien to those reared in the Judeo-Christian cul-

tural tradition. Poets wishing to write haiku in English
had to face these and other challenging problems.

A surprising number of poets in the English-speaking
world have been willing to meet the challenge. Even
some major Anglo-American poets such as Ezra
Pound, W.H.Auden, Allen Ginsberg, and John
Ashberry have attempted to write haiku or haiku-like
poems in English.When Japan Airlines held an international haiku contest in 1964, it received more than
40,000 haiku written by people in every walk of life.
This was the time when I myself became interested in
English haiku. A couple of years later Harold
G.Henderson wrote to me about a plan to establish
the Haiku Society of America. I became a member of
the society when the plan materialised. I also sub-
scribed to all the early haiku magazines, such as
American Haiku and *Haiku West* and tried to buy all
the collections of haiku reviewed in those magazines.
After several years however, I had to give up that
effort because the number of new haiku books
increased at a rate far beyond my expectations.
Fortunately there soon appeared several anthologies of
English haiku, such as Cor Van der Heuvel's *The
Haiku Anthology (1974,1986),* and George Swede's *The
Canadian Haiku Anthology(1979),* which presented the
finest examples of this emerging genre of English poetry. *Global Haiku* is a welcome new addition, especially
since it includes the work of haiku poets living both in
and outside North America. Because of its editorial
policy it has had to exclude a number of noteworthy
poets in the United States and Canada, such as the editors themselves. But their haiku are available in other
anthologies like the two cited above, and the reader of
this volume is urged to consult them. This fact itself is
testimony to the large quantity of good haiku written
in English today.

Obviously the haiku has not yet attained the kind of
status the sonnet occupies in English literature at present. Yet it has only been a few decades since Anglo-
American poets began to write haiku seriously. And,
even though the number is small, some haiku have-
found their way into the canon of English poetry. *The*

Norton Anthology of Modern Poetry(1973), one of the standard college textbooks in North America, contains thirteen poems that are called haiku, in addition to the haiku-like poems of Ezra Pound, Wallace Stevens, and William Carlos Williams. A number of English textbooks for elementary and secondary schools include haiku, either translated from Japanese, or written originally in English. Will there ever be a great English haiku poet who might be compared to a great English sonneteer such as Shakespeare or Spenser? Only time will tell. Who knows - perhaps he or she is is represented in this anthology?

Acknowledgements

The 325 haiku which we selected for Global Haiku were the survivors of several elimination rounds. For the first round, we gathered as many haiku of the 25 contributors as we could find and ended-up with several thousand. To enable us to cope with this overwhelming number, we pressed into service two capable haiku editors and poets, who also happened to be our spouses: Shirley Brooks and Anita Krumins. The four of us met in Decatur, Illinois on August 24, 1997 and over the next three days, from early morning to late at night, selected about 700 haiku that we felt should go on to the second round.

We are very grateful to Shirley and Anita for their considerable help during this stage. We would also like to thank Father Dan Rogers and Tony Virgilio, the literary executors for Raymond Roselip and Nick Virgilio, respectively, for giving us total access to the work of the two deceased poets.

We would also like to express our appreciation to ai li, Andre Duhaime, Lee Gurga, Dorothy Howard and Cor van Heuvel who assisted us in various ways.

The Editors
January 2000

INTRODUCTION

The Background

During the last twenty-five years, eight well-regarded haiku anthologies have been published: Cor van den Heuvel's three versions of *The Haiku Anthology*, the first published in 1974, the second in 1986 and the third in 1999; George Swede's *The Canadian Haiku Anthology* (1979); *Haiku: Anthology Canadienne/Canadian Anthology* (1985) by Dorothy Howard and André Duhaime; *Midwest Haiku Anthology* (1992) by Randy Brooks and Lee Gurga; *The Haiku Hundred* (1992) by James Kirkup, David Cobb and Peter Mortimer; and Bruce Ross's *Haiku Moment* (1993). With the exception of *The Haiku Hundred,* all focused on the work of poets from the United States and Canada.

What distinguishes all of these anthologies from those found in mainstream poetry is that they are non-elitist, including both major and minor haiku poets as well as everyone in-between. As the number of persons writing haiku grew, the number of contributors to each successive anthology mirrored this growth. For instance, van den Heuvel's first anthology has thirty-eight contributors, his second , sixty-six and his third eighty nine, while Ross's collection included one-hundred and eighty-five.

In a paper presented at the 1993 Haiku North America conference I suggested that someone should edit a book that includes only the major haiku poets:

' It is time that the poets who have contributed most in terms of quality and innovation be recognized ... The editor(s) in charge of this project will have to

*have a deep knowledge not only of all the work
published in the haiku periodicals, but also of the
true history of developments in haiku writing. For
instance, who were the most significant poets in
influencing others? Who were the true innovators,
who were the imitators? Who produced the most
haiku of the highest quality, regardless of whether
they were innovators or imitators?'*
(Swede, 1993).

Ironically, that *'someone'* turned out to be me. In
April 1997, Peter Mortimer, a playwright, poet
and editor of England's IRON Press visited
Toronto. During one of our numerous chats
about poetry, I mentioned the need for a 'best'
haiku anthology. He said, ' *Why don't you do it?
If you do, I'll publish the book.'*

The speed of my affirmative reply indicated to
me that I must have subconsciously thought I
could edit such a work. One of Pete's provisos,
to which I readily agreed, was that I could not, as
editor, include my own haiku. His other condi-
tion was that I include poets from around the
world and not limit myself to those from the
U.S. and Canada, places with the longest and
most vital histories of haiku writing and publishing outside Japan. I agreed because strong interest
in the haiku form had emerged in other countries, particularly Great Britain, with the result
that they were producing talented haiku poets
who could easily fit in the anthology I had in
mind.

Less than a week later, I was in Tokyo giving a
paper at a conference jointly sponsored by the
Japanese-based *Haiku International* and the *Haiku
Society of America*. One of the other presenters
was Randy Brooks, a long-time U.S. haiku poet,
editor and publisher. His paper on the history of
North American haiku magazines impressed me

with its detailed knowledge of the haiku scene. In several subsequent talks with Randy, I discovered that his expertise extended to haiku developments in other parts of the world as well. It became apparent to me that me that the IRON Press anthology would be improved if Randy got involved as associate editor.

The Selection of the Twenty-five Poets

From the outset, two criteria informed our choices of the twenty-five poets to be included, the quality and quantity of their work. Many poets write a few good poems, but few poets write many good poems. The few poets are the focus of this anthology.

Of course, a selection process such as this is never quite that straightforward. Two other factors played important roles throughout; the poet's influence on other poets and the poet's country of origin, that is, the nation in which the poet first started to develop his or her talent. The influence factor enabled us to separate poets who were closely matched as far as the quality and quantity criteria were concerned and the nation variable, insisted on by the publisher, became the final strainer through which we put all of our candidates.

Deciding on which poets to include was often gut-wrenching. For each one we put into the anthology, we had to leave out several others who were deserving. Thus, regrettably absent are such significant U.S. haiku poets as *Bob Boldman, L.A. Davidson, Garry Gay, Allen Ginsberg, J.W. Hackett, Lorraine Ellis Harr, William J. Higginson, Clement Hoyt, Foster Jewell, Adele Kenny, Jack Kerouac, Elizabeth Searle Lamb, Michael McClintock, Alan Pizzarelli, Francine Porad, Jane*

Reichhold, Lee J. Richmond, O. Mabson Southard, Robert Spiess, Wally Swist, John Wills, Richard Wright, Ruth Yarrow and Virginia Brady Young. Absent as well are such important Canadians as Eric Amann, Nick Avis, Jack Cain, Michael Dudley, Marco Fraticelli, Dorothy Howard, anne mckay, Ruby Spriggs and Elizabeth St. Jacques.

Also missing are many noteworthy haiku voices from outside North America: Australia's *Janice Bostok*, and Great Britain's *Colin Blundell, Stephen Gill, Michael Gunton, Jackie Hardy, Ken Jones, James Kirkup, Bruce Leeming, George Marsh, Chris Mulhern, Susan Rowley, Fred Schofield, Brian Tasker, Bill Wyatt,* and Ireland's *Jim Norton,* and Japan's *Kris Kondo, Shokan Kondo, Kohjin Sakamoto, Edith Shiffert,* and New Zealand's *Cyril Childs, John O'Connor, Jeanette Stace and Richard von Sturmer.*

The Twenty-Five

Here, in alphabetical order, are the twenty-five haiku poets we selected for this anthology: *ai li (U.K.), David Burleigh (N. Ire./Jap.), David Cobb (U.K.), Margaret Chula (U.S.), Dee Evetts (U.K./U.S.), LeRoy Gorman (Can.), Caroline Gourlay (U.K.), Lee Gurga (U.S.), Penny Harter (U.S.), Cicely Hill (U.K.), Gary Hotham (US/UK), Jean Jorgensen (Can.), Dhugal Lindsay (Aus./Jap.), Martin Lucas (U.K.), Peggy Lyles (U.S.), Marlene Mountain (U.S.), Bill Pauly (U.S.), Raymond Roseliep (U.S.), Alexis Rotella (U.S.), Vincent Tripi (U.S.), Cor van den Heuvel (U.S.), Anita Virgil (U.S.), Nicholas Virgilio (U.S.), Michael Dylan Welch (Can./U.S.), Rod Willmot (Can.).*
The process by which Randy and I selected haiku from these 25 contributors was straightforward;

if we both felt that a work was of high quality, it was included. Of course, we had to limit the number of haiku selected because of space restrictions.

Preceding the haiku selections for each of the 25 poets is a brief biography written by Randy Brooks and I which typically includes basic facts such as year and place of birth,education and occupations.

Each biography also lists the poet's significant published collections. It is from these that we culled the vast majority of the haiku in this anthology. Most of the remainder were previously unpublished pieces the authors submitted to us. The rest had not yet found their way into a collection, but had appeared in one of the following places: *Blithe Spirit, Home: BHS Members Anthology, The Internet, Lynx, Mainichi Daily News, Modern Haiku, Poetry Nippon, Time Haiku.*

George Swede

TOWARDS A DEFINITION OF
THE ENGLISH HAIKU

The haiku originated six to seven hundred years ago in Japan and has grown to become one of the most popular poetic forms in the world. Two explanations for this success are its shortness and seeming simplicity. These characteristics are probably why the haiku is one of the earliest poems taught to children all over the globe.

Of course, composing haiku is not nearly as simple as grade school teachers make out. The skill needed to create consistently excellent haiku takes just as long to acquire as for any other type of poetry. It has been well-documented how *Basho*(1644-1694), arguably the greatest haiku poet ever, reached his peak only after two arduous decades of writing and study (*Yuasa* 1974, *Ueda* 1991).

The haiku involves a number of compositional guidelines with which an aspiring haiku poet must become thoroughly acquainted. As *Yuasa* (1974, 9) reminds us:
'Haiku, like any other form of literature, has grown out of a long process, and it is subject to a number of restrictions historically imposed upon it'.
This does not mean that all the criteria have to be slavishly obeyed. As I will show in this section, some are more in the nature of general norms which can be followed or not. However, there are a number that are essential - the brain, heart and lungs of the haiku's existence.
My method to arrive at a definition of the haiku suitable for the English language was to draw up

a comprehensive list of criteria and then see which ones were considered essential and which expendable as indicated by the published work of English-language haiku poets. To get the list, I scrutinized the definitions of haiku given by the most widely-recognized authorities: *Blyth (1949), Yasuda (1957), Henderson(1958, 1967), Giroux (1974), Yuasa (1974), Ueda 1976, 1991), Higginson(1985) and van den Heuvel (1986).* The result was a total of eight criteria that seemed to encompass every aspect of writing haiku in English.

What follows is a systematic examination of these eight criteria to see which are still meaningful and which have outlived their usefulness. The results will provide us with a new definition of the haiku, one that is more in touch with what English-language poets are really writing

Criterion 1: The Haiku Is a Poem that Is Brief
This criterion has two corollaries:
a It should contain seventeen syllables
b.When spoken, it should be approximately one breath-length long

Criterion number one is universally followed. In whatever form or shape we find the English haiku, in books, magazines and anthologies, it is invariably shorter than practically any other form of poetry. The two corollaries, seventeen syllables and breath length, provide concrete ways to indicate what is meant by 'brief' But even with these apparently simple, objective criteria, differences between Japanese and English create complications.
Japanese syllables, or 'onji', are more uniform than in English, that is, seventeen onji nearly

always take one breath to utter *(Yasuda 1957)*. In contrast, whether seventeen syllables in English can fit comfortably into one breath depends on their length and ease of pronunciation. For example, the following haiku by Nicholas Virgilio and David Cobb both have seventeen syllables, yet Cobb's is harder to say in one breath:

the blind musician
extending an old tin cup
collects a snowflake
(Virgilio 1988, 54)

froth on his whiskers
a man in the pub explains
how high the tide was
(Cobb 1997, 50)

One reason Cobb's haiku takes longer to say is its higher word count, fifteen to Virgilio's eleven. Another is that in Cobb's poem, readers have to make four more brief pauses between successive words in order to make them distinct from one another. A third factor involves ease of line utterance. Cobb uses words with vowel-consonant combinations that take longer to say. The first line of each haiku illustrates this nicely. Virgilio has one difficult word to utter, 'musician', while Cobb has two, 'froth' and 'whiskers' Such divergences among haiku are much less common in Japanese.

In addition to being more uniform than syllables, onji are also on average quite a bit shorter. The reason is that an onji can have no more than one consonant and long vowels count for two onji *(Giroux* 1974, *Higginson* 1985). As a result, the Japanese see more onji than we perceive syllables in the same word. For instance, a haiku with seventeen onji in Japanese will have only half that number of syllables in English. Or, to put it another way, seventeen-syllable English haiku, like the ones by Virgilio and Cobb, will seem inordinately long to the Japanese reader. Still one more way to understand the language differences is to compare the number of words in a haiku. The average 17 onji Japanese haiku has five or six while the typical seventeen-syllable English haiku has twelve or thirteen, omitting articles (*Giroux* 1974).

Most North American haiku poets have long rec-ognized that the seventeen-syllable length was designed for the characteristics of the Japanese language, not the English. Very few seventeen-syllable, English haiku are as effective as those by Virgilio and Cobb. Nearly all tend to be awk-wardly padded with unnecessary words and, like Cobb's, difficult to say in one normal breath.

My research shows that, starting in the 1960s, 80% of the haiku published in the best antholo-gies and periodicals have fewer than seventeen syllables (*Swede and Amann* 1980, *Swede* 1996). Clearly, the first corollary to rule number one is not required as part of the definition of an English- language haiku. The second corollary involving breath-length has become the sole measure of brevity for the vast majority of North American poets.

Criterion 2: The Haiku Should Be Arranged in Three Lines.
This rule has one corollary: The three lines should be arranged in a 5-7-5 syllable count.

Neither this rule nor its corollary are essential. In fact, Japanese haiku almost always have been and continue to be written in one line or rather, column, as the language is usually written vertically. Because Japanese onji are so short, seventeen onji always fit easily into one line or column. On the other hand, a seventeen-syllable haiku in English usually has to be more than one line otherwise it would run off the page, at least in the normal horizontal way the language is written.

Early translators, such as *Basil Hall Chamberlain* and *Lafcadio Hearn*, began to use three lines for the English version of the one-line Japanese poem. They used this form even for translations that could have fit the one-line format because they felt that Western readers would find one-liners too unusual (*Matsuo-Allard* 1977).

The first decoders did have another option - two line translations. Their preference for three-liners is not difficult to figure out. Seventeen syllables cannot be arranged symmetrically in two lines but with three lines the task is easy, five-seven-five. Thus, the three-line rule is not really a classical rule (in the Japanese sense). It is merely a Western invention to accommodate seventeen syllables. Nevertheless, my research shows that ninety percent of North American haiku stick to the three-line rule (*Swede and Amann 1980, Swede 1996*). This persistence is likely due to the fact that most English-language poets find the three-line form a comfortable way to indicate the two short pauses necessary for making the implied comparison between two things or events. The Japanese indicate these pauses without line breaks by using a special grammatical

device called the 'kireji' or a cutting word or suf-
fix (*Higginson 1985, Yasuda 1957*). As William
Higginson (1985, 102) states:
*'In effect, the kireji is a sort of sounded, rather than
merely written, punctuation. It indicates a pause,
both rhythmically and grammatically.'*
While the great majority of English-language
haiku poets use the three-line form, a few experi-
ment with one-line, two-line, visual and vertical
haiku. Here are a few examples showing how,
despite drastic changes in form, something that is
essentially haiku is retained.

 one fly everywhere the heat
(*Mountain in van den Heuvel, 1986, 155*)

chained to the fence
the dog's collar
(*Harter 1987, 8*)

foot
stepcric
ket
(LeRoy Gorman 1979, 52)
As these examples clearly illustrate, haikuness
does not reside in only the seventeen-syllable,
three-line haiku.These criteria should be eliminated from the definition of the English haiku.
More specifically, criterion number one's first
corollary, regarding a seventeen-syllable length
should be eliminated as should the entire criterion number two which includes a three-line form
and a corollary for a five-seven-five syllable
arrangement.
Persons usually first encounter haiku via a school
text or a dictionary which typically define the
form as a short poem with seventeen syllables

arranged in three lines. As I have indicated, these criteria serve little purpose .Unless they are dropped from the definition, newcomers to haiku will expend undue effort struggling to achieve them rather than concentrating on the essence of haiku-the - content.

However, as stated earlier, criterion one's second corollary, regarding breath length, should be kept. It provides a verifiable way to indicate what is meant by brevity. Of course, there are other poetic forms equally short, such as the closely related senryu (a haiku-like poem involving human nature only) as well as the Western epigram. A new definition will need to distinguish the haiku from these other forms. Nevertheless, the criterion of breath length is justifiable by the fact that nearly all the different kinds of haiku written today can be said in one breath length (or less).

Criterion 3: The Haiku Is a Poem which Describes an Experience of Awe or Transcendental Insight

This criterion has always been the sine qua non of haiku composition and continues to be so today. A very short poem without the feeling of awe or 'ahness' is simply not a haiku. Agreement about this criterion appears to be unanimous, both among classical and modern haiku poets. While a sense of awe can also be created by longer poems, such as those of Wordsworth, the method is different. The longer poem builds its effects through an accumulation of images (sometimes dozens) but the haiku uses only two or three. Thus, for the haiku to be effective, it must capture the essence of an experience. And, as Kenneth Yasuda (1957) suggests, this essence is best expressed in one breath length. Of course, a

longer poem may possess striking combinations
of two or three images that have the same effect
as haiku.

A problem remains however to distinguish the
acute awareness or 'ahness' experienced as a
result of a haiku from what is experienced as a
result of other very short poems such as the senryu and epigram. As can be seen from the following examples, the haiku is substantially different:

Epigram

I am His Highness' dog at Kew;
Pray tell me, sir, whose dog are you?
(Alexander Pope in Richardson 1971, 238)

Pope's epigram is a clever put-down. It does not
transcend the world of egotism, it revels in it.
The response it creates in readers is not one of
'ah' but 'aha' - someone got zapped.

Senryu

going through the tunnel:
the girl looks at her reflection
so do I
(Cor van den Heuvel 1992, unpag.)

Van den Heuvel's poem also contains humour,
but it tugs at deeper, more universally-felt feelings than Pope's witticism. The girl is confirming
her appearance as well as her identity in the
clearer reflection provided by the passage
through the tunnel, while van den Heuvel, the
poet-voyeur, can also get a better look yet retain
his anonymity. What adds to the poem's com-
plexity is the tunnel image which hints at other,
darker yearnings in the girl as well as the observ-
er. The senryu certainly offers the reader more of
an 'ah' than 'aha' moment, but it stops short of
the transcendental experience of a haiku:

more darkness
more fireflies
more darkness than fireflies
(Gary Hotham 1988, unpag.)

Hotham's haiku has a greater depth and breadth
of emotion than either the epigram or senryu. In
van den Heuvel's poem, darkness is peripheral to
the humour of the situation, while in Hotham's
darkness is central to the poem and the humour
peripheral. The final line has the humorous ele-
ment, but, ultimately, the humour is overcome
by the universal knowledge of eventual oblivion.
The end result is sadness mixed with awe at the
powerful forces with dominion over us.
The creation of transcendental insight or a sense
of awe is an essential characteristic of the haiku
and one that made Blyth (1949)and others consid-
er it to be a Zen poem. No doubt the feeling of
transcendence a good haiku evokes could be
described by the Zen term 'satori' which Alan
Watts (1960,86) defines as 'awakening to our
original inseparability with the universe'.Haiku
can best be understood as poetry and not part of
Zen or any religious/philosophical outlook.What
provides the haiku with the power to evoke feelings of transcendence? The most important factor seems to be the inclusion of nature which is
also criterion four.

*Criterion 4: The Haiku Is a Poem which Contains
Some Reference to Nature Other than Human
Nature*
This criterion has one corollary: The reference to
nature should involve a season word. Hotham's

haiku has deeper reverberations than van den Heuvel's senryu because it is set within the context of the natural world with its uncontrollable rhythms. As a result it creates a sense of awe or wonder, something we don't get from van den Heuvel's human-made world of subway trains and tunnels. For this reason, a haiku must have nature content, otherwise it is not a haiku, but a senryu.

This is an essential characteristic. Without involving some aspect of nature, a poem cannot be a haiku. While human nature can be part of a haiku, it must occur together with something from the outside world, otherwise the poem becomes a senryu. Compare van den Heuvel's purely human situation with the following haiku by Alexis Rotella which puts a personal dynamic into the context of physical nature:

Waterlilies...
in a moment he'll ask me
what I'm thinking
(Alexis Rotella 1983, 44)

As captivating as van den Heuvel's senryu is, it lacks the expansion of awareness found in Rotella's haiku; it creates fewer ripples of emotion. The inclusion of human concerns within a larger context seems to be vital for generating a feeling of awe, wonder or transcendence. In this same vein, one could argue that Hotham's haiku is even more effective than Rotella's in creating transcendence because it does not mention human beings at all except in an implied manner, that is, the reader knows that the eyes informing the poem are human.

In the well-rendered haiku, the external world

provides an objective correlate to the workings of the inner. In the words of Nobuyuki Yuasa (1974, 33), *'What is remarkable...[is] the symbolism which it achieves without pretending in the least to be symbolic.'* This is the haiku defined in a nutshell.

The corollary to this rule, the need for a season word, stems from the beginnings of the haiku form:

'The haiku has a very specific, historical reason for indicating the season. Haiku originated as the starting verse, or hokku, of the longer renga, or 'linked poem'. Renga were written at parties, by several poets who took turns at writing successive short stanzas. The opening stanza of a renga, the hokku, had a very important function. It had to indicate when the renga was written. Some early hokku had the flavour or newspaper date lines. But subtle poets simply named objects associated with the particular time of year, thus suggesting, rather than stating, the season. The words for these objects came to be known as kigo, or 'season words'.
(Higginson 1985, 90)

The concern with season became so prevalent in Japan that poems were customarily anthologized according to the time of year in which they were set and dictionaries of season words (or kigo) became commonplace. The results of such classification were to be expected - arbitrariness and artificiality (*Blyth 1949, Henderson 1967, Higginson 1985, Yasuda 1957*). For instance, the noun 'haze' has arbitrarily become a standard Japanese season word for spring (*Higginson 1985, Yasuda 1957*). Here is an example of its use in a fine piece by Ryôta, a classical Japanese haiku poet:

From the long hallways
Voices of the people rise
In the morning haze.
(*Ryota in Yasuda 1957, 42*)
But why must readers automatically associate
haze with only spring? I have seen what I would
call haze (as opposed to the thicker and wetter
mist) in summer, fall and winter as well. I have
also seen mist in all four seasons, but season-
word dictionaries relegate mist, as well as fog, to
the autumn (Higginson 1985). While the meaning
of Ryota's haiku will change slightly if haze is
associated with one of the other seasons (or no
season at all), its transcendent quality will
remain constant because what really matters is
the effective juxtaposition of the morning haze
with the rising voices. Many Japanese haiku
poets in the twentieth century, began to rebel
against the dictates of kigo compilations. Makoto
Ueda (1976, 10) quotes a remark made in 1913 by
Ogiwara Seisensui, a major modern Japanese
haiku poet: 'The season word is a fetter fastened
on the living flesh.' Clearly, he was reacting to
the inhibitions on the writer's imagination that
kigo impose. But there are other problems with
season words. Blossoms of several kinds--camel-
lia, double cherry, mountain cherry, thread
cherry, plum--are quintessential Japanese kigo
for spring. Readers living outside Japan, in more
desert or arctic conditions, such as Arizona or
Alaska, are unlikely to see thread cherry blooms
as part of their daily spring experience and thus
will have a reduced appreciation of haiku with
such season words. As a result, poets who use
Japanese kigo will be at a disadvantage with audiences living in these environments. And what
about haiku poets from Arizona and Alaska?

They will have a reduced list of spring kigo from which to draw. Urbanization and controlled environments pose even more difficulties for season words, most of which were compiled in earlier times. For instance, frogs are kigo for spring according to the rationale that this season is the time when their songs are first noticed after a long absence. Quite apart from the issue whether frogs should be season words for spring is the problem that urban dwellers, the vast majority of us, do not normally hear the croaking of frogs in spring or any other time of the year. Thus, this kigo has reduced impact for city audiences plus apartment- dwelling haiku poets have one fewer kigo from which to choose.

In spite of the arguments against the necessity for season words, the majority of Japanese poets continue to use them (Higginson 1985). Knowing this, a small number of North Americans also advocate their use. The leader of the group is William J. Higginson, one of the foremost North American haiku scholars. In 1996, he published two volumes, one that provides a theoretical foundation for the use of seasonal words or topics, *The Haiku Seasons: Poetry of the Natural World*, and the other, an international dictionary of season words, *Haiku World: An International Poetry Almanac.* Of the two, *Haiku World* is the greater achievement, breath- taking in its scope of knowledge about the flora and fauna of the world. It is very useful for fully understanding haiku written by poets living in climates very different from one's own and, especially, when they use unfamiliar animals and plants to connote a season. Here is an indication of Higginson's motivation around the time he started writing the two season books (1985, 94-95):

Conventions arise because many people do the same thing. Many people wrote poems on frogs in the spring, when their singing was first noticed, and therefore most noticeable. Soon it was the fashion to write of frogs in the spring. People who observed-and observe-this fashion do not deny the existence of frogs in the summer. But they express their membership in a special community of human perception by writing of frogs in the spring. As a reader of haiku it seems reasonable to try to know these conventions of season, and to use that knowledge to expand the meanings of haiku written according to them.

What, then, do we conclude about the corollary to rule number four--that haiku must have season words? Are they essential or not? Obviously, the answer is not straightforward. Higginson makes a very strong case for their use. On the other hand, I believe they are not necessary, but neither do they have to be ignored. Many fine haiku clearly indicate the season and many do not. In fact, of the eight haiku used as examples up to this point, only four have content that specifies an unambiguous season, those by Virgilio, Mountain, Gorman and Hotham. Since this is an examination of elements absolutely vital to the definition of haiku, the conclusion is unavoidable--season words are not necessary, although a knowledge of them can be useful, both for the composition of haiku and for the understanding of work written in foreign lands. Up to this point I have discussed the four most commonly-stated criteria and corollaries for haiku composition. Based on what English-language poets are actually publishing, my conclusions are to drop criterion number one's first corollary requiring

seventeen syllables, to eliminate criterion number two (the three-line form) as well as its corollary (a five-seven-five arrangement) and to dis-
pense with the fourth criterion's corollary about
season words. However, it seems imperative to
retain criterion one's second corollary about
brevity as defined by breath length as well as criterion three which is concerned about 'ahness'
and criterion four which expresses the need for
nature content.

Criterion 5: The Haiku Is a Poem which Involves Sense Images; It Does Not Involve Generalizations

This characteristic is also essential and follows so
inevitably from rule four that many definitions
do not mention it. Nevertheless, from my experience giving writing workshops, I have found that
stating this criterion outright seems to provide
the necessary focus for many students. Readers
require definite objects juxtaposed in a believable
manner otherwise they cannot extrapolate effec-
tively from the depicted event to their own existence. To illustrate, here is a haiku that fails to
communicate because it involves abstract ideas
rather than tangible things:

time
is what
is still
(Raymond Roseliep 1980a, 46)

The meaning of 'time' is not pinned down by
reference to something specific. Thus, Roseliep's
three lines remain more of an intellectual exercise
than anything else. Readers have only a fuzzy
notion of what the poet is trying to say and

would have to create their own images to make more sense of his lines. Roseliep might be the best as well as the most influential poet in this anthology and thus it is not surprising that he has written another haiku on time in which everything works the way it should:

Spring breeze
puffs through the skeleton
of a bird
(Roseliep 1980b, 6)

How much more effective the second haiku is! With vivid images Roseliep operationalizes what he means by time - in this case the arrival of spring and the possibilities of rebirth after winter, the season of death. Of course, readers will depart from this surface meaning in their own ways. But the places from which they leave will be much more palpable than they were in Roseliep's failed poem on time and their inner experiences ultimately will be richer and more transcendent.

Criterion 6: The Haiku Is a Poem which Presents an Event as Happening Now, Not in the Past or in the Future

Like the previous rule, this criterion is rarely stated openly. It is simply assumed that the present tense is the one that will maximize the haiku's experience for readers. In the published literature, almost no Japanese or North American haiku exist in another tense. It is also the only rule about which I have not had a consistent opinion. Years ago I argued that a skilled poet could achieve immediacy by using the past tense *(Swede 1984, 9)*. The example I gave was this haiku by Raymond Roseliep:

I whispered of death
one winter night in a voice
we both never knew
(Roseliep, 1977, 36)

Today, I have changed my mind. The past tense
does precisely what it is supposed to do
bring readers to an earlier time. Immediacy has
definitely been lost. As such it is not a haiku but
a short poem involving reminiscence. I wonder
why Roseliep allowed this piece to be published
as a haiku. With only slight modifications, of
which he was very capable, Roseliep could have
achieved the required immediacy for a true
haiku. I have taken the liberty to make the
changes of which he very likely would have
approved (he died in 1983):

Winter night
I whisper of death in a voice
we both do not know

The result is the essence or special 'ahness' characteristic of haiku. True, I have altered the meaning somewhat, but readers should feel more
deeply the feelings associated with the recogni-
tion of our mortality than in the original version which asks for identification with a more
distant memory of the occasion. What is ironic
about this discussion is that all haiku are essentially memories which the poet relates as present
events. In essence, the poet is lying, but we pre-
fer to regard the lies as imaginative reinterpreta-
tions or reinventions of reality.

Criterion 7: The Haiku Is a Poem which Is

Objective, that is, It Expresses as Little as Possible of the Poet's Personality

This rule is unnecessary. If the essential rules discussed so far are followed, then the haiku has very little room left for the poet's personality to be expressed. But that small space that remains can be filled with a few artfully disclosed personal items that will add to the richness of the impression a haiku makes. Anyone knowledgable about the history of haiku can distinguish most of the work of the classical masters from one another. The usual choice of words and their arrangement, the preference for certain topics over others, the presence or absence of humour, and so on, all reveal something about the person behind the poems. Rod Willmot (1980, 33-34) takes even a more definite position: 'acute observations of suchnesses is [sic] not enough... there must be a sense of the man behind the work, the shaping personality that has itself been shaped by experience'.

Criterion 8: The Haiku Is a Poem which Usually Avoids Poetic Devices such as Metaphor, Rhyme, Etc.

This rule is also unnecessary. Haiku are, after all poetry. Furthermore, there are many examples of the restrained use of poetic devices in both classical and modern haiku. No one would deny that this poem by the classical master Buson captures an acute moment of awareness in spite of metaphor and hyperbole:

About to bloom,
and exhale a rainbow,
The peony
(Buson in Roseliep 1976, 20)

Another successful use of metaphor occurs in this modern haiku by Caroline Gourlay:

Writing at my desk,
I look out across the sea...
 words slip their moorings
(Gourlay 1995, 21)

In the third line, the reader associates words with boats or ships because of the nautical terms 'slip' and 'moorings'. Once the reader makes this comparison, the word moorings itself becomes a metaphor for whatever Gourlay was focused on writing, probably a poem. The reader readily accepts these comparisons because the sea is the centre of the poem, both figuratively and literally. Gourlay's metaphor is complex and fully-integrated and actually intensifies the moment she is describing.

Rhyme is a device which, if not used carefully, will draw too much attention to itself and, consequently, undermine the experience of a haiku's meaningful moment. However, when employed economically and skilfully, rhyme can sometimes enhance the experience:

the bones of a bird
on the spring path of lovers
not saying a word
(Raymond Roseliep 1979, 31)

Roseliep's rhyme is easy to miss because it occurs naturally with the words most suited to the description of the moment. Any other kind of rhyme in haiku will be a burden, for the poem is too small to carry the weight. What must be remembered about all poetic devices is that their overuse can weaken the central life, not only of a haiku, but of any other form of poetry as well. Their use must be spare and meaningful; their goal to heighten the moment of insight and make it memorable.

In Summation, Only Five Rules Remain Essential

In summary, this examination of the eight classical criteria reveals only five which still remain crucial today:

1. The haiku must be brief, that is, when read aloud it should be one breath-length long.

2. The haiku must express a sense of awe or transcendent insight.

3. The haiku must involve some aspect of nature other than human nature.

4 The haiku must possess sense images, not generalizations.

5. The haiku must present an event as happening now, not in the past or in the future

Nothing absolute exists about the three criteria and the three corollaries that I have dropped. Unlike the five essential criteria, their presence or absence does not create or destroy a haiku. Whether or not they are followed becomes a matter of personal choice. Almost thirty years ago, Henderson (1967, 42) drew the following conclusions about the state of the English haiku:

There is as yet no complete unanimity among American poets (or editors) as to what constitutes a haiku in English - how it differs from other poems which may be equally short. In other words, haiku in English are still in their infancy'.

Perhaps today, these five defining criteria may create, if not total, at least greater unanimity. The haiku in English is growing up. The suggestion that we part with some of the traditional rules is by no means unique to English-language haiku. The history of the Japanese haiku (especially in the twentieth century) is full of experimentation and controversy (Higginson 1985). Coexisting in Japan today are various schools of haiku poets ranging from the traditionalist to the free-form experimentalist (Ueda 1976). What all this activity on both sides of the world shows is the tremendous versatility and vitality of the haiku form.

George Swede

ai li

a lock of hair
on the mortician's table
still golden

*

by the bed
teeth in a glass
night companion

*

in christmas snow
the only footprints
mine

*

rusty daimler
alighting dowager
farts

*

empty nursery . . .
stick-on stars
still glowing

mother
listening to rain
in father's bed

*

rain disperses crowd
two deck chairs
alone again

*

washing up
for one
snow falling

*

the morning after
a bowl of cereal
quietly crunched

*

moon over key largo
the one i'm with
watching the small screen

water trough
a horse
drinking sky

*

the man who loved her
his son sends
a wreath

*

amusement park
the poster of
a missing child

*

a palm open
for friendship
the lifeline short

David Burleigh

A sudden downpour
brings them to the bookshop -
schoolboys all in white

*

A New Testament
forgotten on a college bench -
spring zelkova

*

A night with no wind
to stir the chimes - a clinking
of ice in glasses

*

The door flung back -
snow falling on the garden
in a soft gray light

*

Hanging new curtains -
blooms already showing on
the persimmon tree

A burning red line
under the wingtip.- sunrise
on the equator

*

A ball in springtime
making its way downriver
slowly to the sea

*

The morning paper--
I set down my coffee cup
in Argentina

Margaret Chula

this early heat
        a carp arches
into the raindrops

*

in strawmat raincoats
farmers plant rice
their boots croaking

*

returning
the borrowed umbrella
splattered with blossoms

*

sawing afternoon
into evening
cicadas

*

old man speaks
the breath
        before the sound

lying side by side
separate letters
from our divorced friends

*

hibachi embers -
red berries
dusted with snow

*

on the second floor
corpse
with the night light on

*

long winter night
    tangerine peels
        piling up

*

sudden shower
in the empty park
    a swing still swinging

they have discovered
my flowered kimono
those relentless ants

*

how hard the gravestone
an ant disappears
into the crevice

David Cobb

where knights lived -
wormholes in the timbers
shedding no more dust

*

a whiff of horse muck -
the name of the famous poet
just escapes me

*

strung roof to roof
on something invisible -
doves in the fog

*

darkening mere -
a heron coils its neck
the last half inch

*

shelter from the rain -
the gardener pees
in his watering can

barbecue -
hairs on the cook's belly
sprinkled with salt

*

froth on his whiskers
a man in the pub explains
how high the tide was

*

after the all-clear
not remembering the bombs
only the kiss

*

daily we meet:
always she wears a smile
going the other way

*

convent - on the line
a nun's black stockings
slap across my face

breakfast in silence--
both halves of the grapefruit
unsweetened

*

flu convalescent
craning for apple buds
a flight of finches

*

first hint of spring -
a thin snake half emerges
to be poked with sticks

*

whelks
all over the beach
auntie's bunions

*

umbrella'd lovers--
the rain falling briefly
on both their backs

Dee Evetts

unexpected news
she stands staring into
the cutlery drawer

*

night of the meteors
we come in
with aching necks

*

with a flourish
the waitress leaves behind
rearranged smears

*

on the freeway
discussing the chocolate bar
in the trunk

*

loud applause
for the last speech
before lunch

on the nude beach
not noticing her until
she puts on a blouse

*

rainy night
        half the cat
still indoors

*

friends from the south
a giant bowl of strawberries
in the midnight dusk

*

first days of summer
    left hand wrist deep
    in a jar of beans

*

her smile
almost a woman's
extended by chocolate

LeRoy Gorman

tubal or vasectomy?
we buy the kids
balloons

*

halfmast
the flag
against the green leaves

*

in the raw
she eats an apple
first

*

her father's coffin lowered
　　behind me
　　a cough

*

no thunder
the cow lets down
　her milk

a diver brings up the body

the rain
begins

*

she dresses

under her arm
the moon

*

false labor
the nurse rearranges
flowers

*

child missing
billboard girl
on a swing

*

sleepless nite
    the mousetrap
    snap

a car passes overhead
    the plunk
    of the baited hook

*

foot
stepcric
ket

*

spla
rrribit
sh

*

stone   skip . . . . tone   skips

*

getting louder
the calf
the auctioneer

*

beyond the laughing billboard girl
a hang-glider
in the sun

*

my family asleep
I worry about money & count
fireflies in our garden

*

during the sermon
I clean the week
from my nails

Caroline Gourlay

Daylight fading -
a curlew's cry
lengthens the hill

*

left behind
by the young couple
this warm stone

*

Quaker meeting
breaking the silence
rain at the window

*

the last guest leaves--
a rose
opens in the vase

*

finished picture -
the violet dead now
in the saucer

butterflies in the catmint -
the old woman's hands
cannot settle . . .

*

delayed homecoming -
the moon wanders
from room to room

*

in the small gap
between the quivering nettles -
a rabbit's still eye

*

Spring won't bring you back.
I watch a flight of wild geese,
both feet on the ground.

*

Writing at my desk,
I look out across the sea -
words slip their moorings.

Barn door swinging shut,
the darkness left inside
until next summer.

*

Without full stop
you run. Childhood, a country
with no paragraphs

Lee Gurga

morning twilight . . .
horse asleep in the pasture
covered with frost

*

pine shade
the wooden bench
worn smooth

*

night sounds . . .
I put another blanket
on the sleeping boy

*

the ticking of sleet
on the bedroom window;
your hand
gathers
me

*

opossum bones
wedged in an upper fork
budding leaves

*

summer morning -
a withered bluebell
loggers left behind

*

frozen branches
measure the emptiness -
winter sunset

*

figure drawing class -
in the model's deepest shadows
a stark white string

*

graduation day
my son & I side by side
knotting our ties

his side of it
her side of it.
winter silence

*

now that you've left -
your side of the bed covered
with open books

Penny Harter

closed bedroom door -
her shadow darkens
the crack of light

*

Fishing boats rock in place,
their lines floating dark
into the sky.

*

moonlight gleaming
on the grapes - the lovers
can't stop laughing

*

evening rain -
in the froth of the waterfall
pale petals

*

the cat's eyes glitter
as the lizard plays dead
in its mouth

chained to the fence
the dog's collar

*

between the rafters
a dried bird's nest -
the hollow egg

*

in from the cold -
only my hands
to warm my hands

*

the old woman
brushing gray hair
until it sparks

*

thawing
the dead field mouse
opens its mouth

Cicely Hill

from the skylight
the shadow of a bird's wing
  crosses her breast

*

  the branch he cuts
to make a donkey goad
  still in bloom

*

  sundown
over the hillside graveyard
  thin dogs creep away

*

  at dawn
wakened by the long silence
  of an unwound clock

*

  midnight lightning:
neighbor never seen before -
  there, at her window

music in the park
the young girl's yawn reveals
the roof of her mouth

*

they turn to sleep
a moth in the lantern
fluttering still

*

winter market
fish glittering in the sun -
her chilblained heels

*

stairs creak
down in the darkened room a disc
plays itself out

Gary Hotham

one hand
then the other
eating alone

*

sun & moon
in the same sky
the small hand of my wife

*

the only sounds
are distant sounds -
a path through the snow

*

letting
the dog out -
the stars out

*

distant thunder -
the dog's toenails click
against the linoleum

home early -
your empty coat hanger
in the closet

*

where the wind goes
behind the fence
the dog barks

*

another day of snow
the statue's fingers
broken off

*

a pile of orange peelings -
the night watchman
away from his desk

*

more darkness
more fireflies -
more darkness than fireflies

the newborn yawns -
her hands don't go
far

*

the clouds bunch quietly -
I wait alone
after missing the bus

*

between the rocks
water the ocean
didn't take back

*

the doctor's office still air -
my name written down
as I spell it

*

to hear them
walking more slowly

leaves falling

morning fog
not seeing far
the fern's underside

*

yesterday's paper
in the next seat -
the train picks up speed

*

off and on rain -
the long way
home

Jean Jorgensen

dirt-ingrained snow -
children at the bus stop
exchange cigarettes

*

in a darkened room . . .
while a migraine dissipates
scent of summer rain

*

tracing old names
for a class reunion
        leaves in the wind

*

evening prayer
   her fingers slowly examine
   the remaining breast

*

a jet of flame
as the logs crumble
        his hand on her thigh

welts across her face
     tomorrow he'll return
     to breaking horses

*

cool summer evening
     walking
          ahead of a gun

*

chill in the air
     taking her turn at hopscotch
     new kid on the block

*

she tries to fit the child
onto her swollen belly
     fragrance of baking bread

*

prairie churchyard
     lilacs full grown at the head
     of the infant's tombstone

Dhugal Lindsay

clustered magnolia
pouring milk, gushing it
into my throat

*

face-to-face before the jellyfish/
upon my palm . . . my eyeballs

*

a married couple
argues as if spitting out
watermelon seeds

*

lucky to be born
without The Draft over my head
i slash at parsley

*

the walnut
shatters . . .
i'm sure i fret too much

only removed
when he talks with Rover . . .
sunglasses

*

picking up a jellyfish . . .
my lifeline
clear and deep

*

employment found . . .
spaghetti boiled
to softness

Martin Lucas

Horton station:
hidden in the kissing gate
stinging nettles

*

with the evening air
aroma of pipe tobacco
the train is late

*

long shadows
through the quiet schoolyard
the killdeer's cry

*

  somewhere
    between
Giggleswick and Wigglesworth
     I am uninspired

*

a public callbox--
while an old man phones, his dog
looks out at the rain

sun on the canal:
a floating football
slowly turning

*

poetry group
deep in thought:
gurgle of plumbing

*

I read my reviews
a funeral procession
passes in silence

Marlene Mountain

```
                 o
                    o
 o            t uch-me-n t
    o         o
                    o       o
          o  o
    o
          o
```

                    *

on this cold
spring 1
2 night 3 4
kittens
wet
5
                    *

grandmother's old quilt
a spot of blood
that won't wash out

                    *

snowy night

from the dripping tap

a glass full

*

new year's
i wear my oldest gown
to bed

*

at dusk hot water from the hose

(In order to print Marlene Mountain's one-line haiku full-out, her work on the next three pages is laid out vertically)

gosling following its neck to the bug

*

old woodcutter rests on the rings of the oak

*

acid rain less and less i am at one with nature

*

you cup my breasts i tablespoon you

*

a late monarch your fingers slowly find my folds

mountain tip from mist my clitoris rises to your mouth

*

is it you or the mountain i am wet in my jeans

*

you harden march blows through the partly opened window

*

together as we dry there is the listening to rain

*

your hand under your shirt finds me

last touch hand on the cold doorknob

*

one fly everywhere the heat

*

autumn evening after splitting wood his wedge

*

autumn dusk the crooked road home

Bill Pauly

after the wake:
cleaning the eyes
of her doll

*

country field
home run rolling
past the headstones

*

snowmelt . . .
she enters
the earth on her knees

*

ten below zero:
man and boy walk through their/
                              breath
to read old tombstones

*

sound of her voice
carrying eggs
across the ice

milkweed pods
swish of her nightsilk
falling

*

white undersides
of birch leaves in the storm
undressing each other

*

fish on their lines rocking /
the rowboat making love

Peggy Lyles

Mother--daughter
　small talk . . .
　　snap beans

*

October twilight:
the scarecrow in the garden
drops its other glove

*

a mayfly
taps the screen -
warm beets slip their skins

*

long twilight . . .
at the woman's ear
a small pearl glows

*

dog-eared script
I prompt a wiseman
from the wings

Winter night:
a spark between the tweeds
of strangers

*

Reaching for green pears -
the pull
of an old scar

*

Offertory chant:
in the darkened vestibule
umbrellas drip

Raymond Roseliep

boiling beet tops
      only for the scent
      Papa loved

*

by hearth light
      gold the white hair
      of his grumbling wife

*

sitting in air
a crow on something
snowed on

*

the banker
cancels
a moth

*

in water
my body
of water

armload of child
unloaded . . .
    the weight of night

*

    the fly rocks
in the spider's hammock
    wide awake

*

the black hen
eating outside
her shadow

*

the firefly you caught
lights the church you make
with your hands

*

I tried to bring you
that one cloud
in this cup of water

campfire extinguished,
the woman washing dishes
in a pan of stars

*

with his going
the birds go
nameless

*

never expecting
the lilies in November
nor the small coffin

*

bathwater
down the drain
some of me

*

grass
holding the shape
of our night

closing the blind
against the day:
this light within

*

telephone wire:
crows are sitting
on her voice

*

walking in rain
I pass a stranger
I know

*

for a moment
the spark
is itself

*

the child is gone
    the paper bell he made
    cracks the wind

Alexis Rotella

canoe through the waterlilies
　　his eyes measuring
　　　　her waist

*

left to the wind
all the lilies
and all his lies

*

wild touch-me-nots:
you never
touch me

*

Just friends:
he watches my gauze dress
blowing on the line

*

You bring me tea
as if everything
were perfect

Leading him in . . .
my bracelet
jangling.

*

morning
the scent of my musk
still on his fingers

*

First spring day
tricycles gather
at the hilltop

*

The priest comes
to bless the house
tracking mud

*

Lunchtime breeze:
computer print-out sheets
sail gently through the park

Undressed:
today's role dangles
from a metal hanger

*

Phone call
his three-day stubble
scraping the distance

*

Discussing divorce
he strokes
the lace tablecloth

*

Late August
I bring him the garden
in my skirt

*

Grandmother's lace gown:
I lift it from the suds
in shreds

Twenty years since prom night,
his face at my front door
beaming

*

Waterlilies . . .
in a moment he'll ask me
what I'm thinking

*

in his wedding band watching/
the clouds pass

*

starrynightIenteryourmirror

*

His footsteps in the room
above me: slowly
I brush my hair

Vincent Tripi

Winter evening -
    grandma's recipe for bread
      among my poems

*

Snow again
    in my cabin somehow
      knowing it is Christmas

*

Moth outside -
    the midwife works
      by candlelight

*

Splashed across
    a thousand years of growth ring
      spotted owl egg

*

The turtle's plash
    just around the bend
      a river Baptism

Letting
     the cat in
     the fog in

*

Farmer's Market -
her cucumber
longer than mine

*

Owl feather
    in my palm
        --the feel of moonlight

Cor van den Heuval

after posting the letter
staring at the slot -
winter rain

*

the spring marsh
a lost decoy floats out
of a side channel

*

the wind
along the old railroad tracks
a milkweed pod opens

*

going through the tunnel:
the girl looks at her reflection
so do I

*

in the mirrors on her dress
little pieces of my
self

a masked doctor
pushes an empty wheelchair
along the corridor

*

high above the city
dawn flares
from a window-washer's pail

*

by the lawn's edge
the dog barks at the darkness
then looks back at me

*

a torn-up girlie magazine
at the end of the woods road
it begins to rain

*

the batter looks
at the placement of his feet
as the strike goes by

lonely night
the faces painted on the windows
of a toy bus

*

in her dressing room
the stripper powders her breasts
and whispers something to them

*

misty rain
confetti sticks to the hoofs
of the parading horses

*

after the speeches
the honored dead return
to their silence

*

dark road
sparks from a cigarette
bounce behind a car

Anita Virgil

behind sunglasses
I doze and wake . . .
the friendly man talks on

*

not seeing
the room is white
until that red apple

*

holding you
in me still . . .
sparrow songs

*

2 fat broads
the photographer grabs
his wide-angle lens

*

hot afternoon . . .
only the slap slap
of a jump rope

thru the hospital gown
your shoulder
small as our child's

*

she turns the child
to brush her hair
with the wind

*

spring breeze . . .
   her breasts sway
over the porcelain tub

*

hot afternoon . . .
the dripping beaks
of slow swans

*

Darkening
the cat's eyes:
a small chirp

that moment
when the night clouds give back
a star

*

when the guests leave
the old cat
purrs & purrs

*

frozen grass . . .
steam from a turd rises
toward the morning stars

*

rainy Sunday
cooped up the puppy gently gnaws
her hind foot

*

the empty slave shack
collapsed
August heat thickens

Nicholas Virgilio

lily:
out of the water . . .
out of itself

*

the graduation ring
slips from my finger:
the midnight river

*

another autumn:
still silent in his closet
father's violin

*

the knifegrinder's bell
fades in the afternoon heat:
cicada

*

between tricks knitting booties

Thanksgiving alone:
ordering eggs and toast
in an undertone

＊

my dead brother
wearing his gloves and boots
I step into deep snow

＊

shadowing hookers
after dark:
the cross in the park

＊

alone on the road
in the wake of the hearse
dust on my shoes

＊

making up her face,
lighting a candle to Mary
for business' sake

the sack of kittens
sinking into the icy creek,
increases the cold

*

winter evening:
leaving father's footprints
I sink into deep snow

*

fossilence
*

the blind musician
extending an old tin cup
collects a snowflake

*

flag-covered coffin:
the shadow of the bugler
slips into the grave

Thanksgiving dinner:
placing the baby's high chair
in the empty space

*

in the single's bar
magnifying loneliness:
her thick eye glasses

*

Viet Nam monument
darkened by the autumn rain:
my dead brother's name

*

my dead brother . . .
hearing his laugh
in my laughter

*

autumn tornado
buckles the billboard:
her torn smile

always returning
to the terminal patient's toe
autumn fly

*

the first snowfall:
down the cellar staircase
my father calls

Michael Dylan Welch

After the quake
the weathervane
pointing to earth

*

after the quake
    a hobo
directing traffic

*

after the quake
    adding I love you
        to a letter

*

toll booth lit for Christmas
from my hand to hers
warm change

*

clicking off the late movie . . .
the couch cushion
reinflates

empty silo -
spring wind pops the metal
in and out

*

home for Christmas:
my childhood desk drawer
empty

*

old folks' home ---
    the square of light
        crosses the room

*

spring breeze -
the pull of her hand
as we near the pet store

*

nursing home lounge -
a child's puzzle
left unfinished

Rod Willmot

Listening . . .
After a while,
   I take up my axe again

*

A page of Shelley
brightens and dims
      with passing clouds

*

her hand on the doorknob
sunlight streams
between her legs

*

she wrings out her blouse
oat-field steaming
after rain

*

the cat between our legs we start/
                     again

she hugs me from behind
my face in the steam
of the potatoes

*

the talk turns to mothers
tomato seeds
spill from her knife

*

humiliated again
bar-smoke in the sweater
I pull from my head

*

on my thirtieth push-up
a dustball
puffs into the air

*

looking away from each other
tick of sleet
on the car roof

abortion clinic
backing away from their shouts
she stumbles

*

paddling slowly
through the reeds
that touch her hair

*

back with more wine
and leaves
on her shoes

*

coming harder than ever thinking/
                    I hate you

*

I watch her close her eyes
a fishbone somewhere
in her mouth

cool cellar
light string somewhere
spiderwebs softly rip

*

water strider
bending the water
where the paddle bends

A HISTORY OF THE ENGLISH HAIKU

The haiku originated in Japan about six to seven hundred years ago and thus is one of the world's oldest surviving poetic forms (*Henderson 1958*). However, the English-speaking world did not learn of its existence until after 1868 when Japan opened its shores to the West and envoys from England started to translate the form (*Giroux 1974*).

A short while later, French visitors to Japan took up writing haiku and in 1905 published an anthology of their work in France. Then, in 1910, two anthologies of Japanese literature in translation were published, one in France and one in England and both included haiku (*Higginson 1985*). While these anthologies created little general interest, they did catch the attention of a much-heralded group of English and American poets headquartered in London and in Chicago between 1910 and 1917 who called themselves the *Imagists* and who took a special interest in the haiku (*Pratt 1963*). Its members, among whom were such luminaries as James Joyce, D.H. Lawrence, Amy Lowell, Marianne Moore, Ezra Pound, Carl Sandburg and William Carlos Williams, used the haiku as a model (along with the classical Greek lyric and French symbolism of the vers libre type) for what they considered to be the ideal poem, ("one in which the image was not a means but an end: the image was not a part of the poem; it was the poem") (*Pratt 1963, 29*). While the Imagists thought of the haiku as an ideal, none of them quite managed to ever write a true one. Pound's famous 'In A Station Of The Metro' is often described as a haiku by persons with only a tenuous knowledge of the form:

The apparition of these faces in the/ crowd;
Petals, on a wet black bough.
(*in Pratt 1963, 50*)

Successful as a short poem, it fails as a haiku because only the first line deals with an immediate experience while the second line involves the memory of an image that the poet uses overtly as a metaphor. As I will elaborate later, a haiku is a haiku because all the images it conveys occur simultaneously in a per son's present perceptions of the world. Thus, to become a haiku, Pound's poem would have to indicate that he saw the faces at the same time as he saw the actual petals in the flesh, not in memory.

In 'Tsai Chih,' Pound comes much closer to the spirit of a true haiku:

The petals fall in the fountain,
the orange-colored rose leaves,
Their ochre clings to the stone.
(*in Pratt 1963, 58*)

Here he manages to deal only with things perceived in a particular moment, but fails to achieve the needed brevity(in the definition chapter) defined as a comfortable breath-length).

W.J. Higginson *(1985, 52)* considers 'Autumn Haze' by Amy Lowell to be 'one of the best hokku [haiku] by a self-styled Imagist':

Is it a dragonfly or a maple leaf
That settles softly down upon the/
    water?

However, this haiku has the same problem as Pound's 'Tsai Chih' - it is too wordy. In sum, while the Imagists saw the haiku as a model for their aspirations, they wrote pieces that were either too metaphorical or too wordy and usually both.

After the Imagist movement broke up around 1917 (*Pratt 1963*), North American interest in the haiku per se languished for several decades until after World War II. Scholars such as Higginson (1985) and Thomas Lynch (1989)have tried to trace the path of the form during this period of more than thirty years and suggest that a continuing interest in the haiku way of seeing was kept alive by the work of a few major poets who made their mark during this time, such as William Carlos Williams (beyond his Imagist days), Wallace Stevens and Charles Reznikoff. Williams' 1923 poem '*The Red Wheelbarrow*' is most often quoted as evidence:

So much depends
upon
a red wheel
barrow
glazed with rain
water
beside the white
chickens
(*Williams 1958, 37*)

As *Lynch (1989, 141)* states, 'All that keeps this poem from being an excellent haiku is the opening two lines, which by haiku standards are quite unnecessary.'

To this editorial comment, I would add that the title is also superfluous. Almost all haiku stand by themselves because a title would normally detract from the desired effect. The poem itself typically conveys all that is important and the reader can capture this at a glance because the haiku is so brief.

Both Higginson and Lynch also single out Wallace Stevens' *Thirteen Ways of Looking at a Blackbird*' as proof of the haiku's influence: The first stanza of the thirteen composing the poem is the most frequently quoted:

Among twenty snowy mountains,
The only moving thing
Was the eye of the blackbird.
(*Stevens 1971, 20*)

As with Williams' '*The Red Wheelbarrow*,' only a small change is necessary to make this a true haiku. As it stands, it lacks the immediacy required in a haiku, but this can easily be remedied by dropping the verb 'was.' 'Thirteen Ways of Looking at a Blackbird' was first published in 1917,

during the last year of the Imagist movement. Thus, the poem might simply
have been the young Stevens' lone exper-
iment with haiku-like poetry. But we
can find similar writing in later work
such as this stanza from the 1936 'A
Postcard from the Volcano':

At what we saw. The spring clouds/
blow
Above the shuttered mansion-house,
Beyond our gate and the windy sky
(*Stevens 1971, 127*)

Nevertheless, such direct images are rare
in the more maturework of Stevens
which is richly metaphorical in the best
tradition of Western poetry.

On the other hand, Charles Reznikoff
did show a steady kinship with the haiku
way of seeing throughout his long
career as *Geoffrey O'Brien (1982, 21)*

points out:

Reznikoff wrote in a variety of forms . . .
but most typically he employed brief lyrical
forms, often grouping short units into such
comfortably loose sequences as
'Autobiography:New York' and

'*Autobiography: Hollywood*', sequences
*which do not rise toward a climax or seek
an overall symbolic meaning but rather
collect a series of powerful moments related
only by their position in the author's experience."*
Here is one of his poems that needs no
editing to become a true haiku:

About an excavation
a flock of bright red lanterns
has settled.
(*in O'Brien 1982, 20*)

However, most of Reznikoff's work is
composed of haiku-like lines imbedded
in longer stanzas. The reader has to
pluck them out like brilliantly coloured
feathers from a peacock. Here, for
instance, are the last two lines from a
five-line stanza:

From the bare twigs
rows of drops like shining buds are
hanging
(*in O'Brien, 1982, 20*)

Nevertheless, compared to Williams and
Stevens, Reznikoff is probably the
strongest strand spanning the years
between the Imagists and the 1950s, a
decade which *E.S. Lamb (1979a, 5)*

describes as the 'real beginning of what may be called the haiku movement in the western world.'

The chief reason for the renewed interest was American fascination with Japanese culture following World War II. In particular, artistic and intellectual Americans became enthralled with Zen whose history as well as charm *Bullock and Stallybrass (1977, 682)* succinctly explain:

Zen [is] the Japanese version of the Ch'an sect of Buddhism in China, noted for its simple austerity, its mysticism leading to personal tranquillity, and its encouragement of education and art. Some of its scriptures and paintings have become widely known and admired in the West; and Aldous Huxley and others in California led something of a cult of Zen, which in the 1960s began appealing to students as a way of having religious experience without dogmas or religious institutions.

For many, this interest grew to encompass Japanese art and literature. As a result, the haiku translations of scholars H.G. Henderson (1934, 1958) and R.H. Blyth (1949) began to be widely read (Lamb 1979a). Blyth's four volume

Haiku became especially popular at this time because his translations were based on the assumption that the haiku was the poetic expression of Zen. Not surprisingly, his books attracted the attention of the Beat school, most notably writers such as Allen Ginsberg, Gary Snyder and Jack Kerouac, all of whom had a prior interest in Zen. All three wrote haiku as well as about haiku. Kerouac, especially, played a huge role in popularizing the form. In fact, his book, "*The Dharma Bums* became the bible to a whole generation of American youth. It introduces the reader to 'Japhy Ryder' a character based on Gary Snyder. Japhy writes haiku and suddenly so do a lot of other people. Several of the poets I [*Higginson*] know first discovered the haiku in Kerouac's novel." (*Higginson 1985, 64*).

While the Beats' interest in the haiku contributed greatly to its widespread acceptance, only Kerouac and Ginsberg wrote in the form long enough to eventually produce small bodies of work. Kerouac (1971) published twenty-six haiku in the last four pages of his seventy-six page collection *Scattered Poems* and he collaborated with Albert Saijo and Lew Welch on a prose and haiku diary of a car trip across the U.S. in 1959 which was eventually published as a slim book in 1973 entitled *Trip Trap: Haiku along the Road fromSan Francisco to New York (Ungar 1982)*. Ginsberg published haiku here and there throughout his long career and in 1978 produced *Mostly Sitting Haiku* which was the first collection, albeit small, of haiku by a major U.S. poet *(Lamb 1979a)*.

A study of the haiku written by these two Beats reveals a good grasp of the form. These two pieces, probably from the late fifties or early sixties, successfully evoke fleeting moments of heightened awareness full of metaphorical resonances:

The summer chair
  rocking by itself
In the blizzard

(Jack Kerouac 1971, 74)

I didn't know the names
of the flowers - now
my garden is gone.
(Allen Ginsberg in Higginson 1985, 59)

For Ginsberg, and especially Kerouac, the haiku was a brief diversion from the other writing on which their reputations as well as incomes were based. Time spent on haiku meant time away from their bread and butter. Nevertheless, in the history of the haiku movement they play a significant role.

Around the same time that the Beats were exploring the haiku, so was an American novelist and poet from an earlier generation, RichardWright. Apparently while sick and bed-ridden in Paris in 1959, he read Blyth's four-volume Haiku and 'discovered in it something he had been unconsciously seeking to ease his mind' (*Michel Fabré as cited in Lynch 1989, 144*). The result was an output much larger than that of either Kerouac or Ginsberg - about 4,000 haiku which he sifted down to a manuscript of 817 entitled This Other World which was recently published(Wright 1998). As with the work of Ginsberg and Kerouac, Wright's best haiku reach high standard:

> Coming from the woods
A bull has a lilac sprig
> Dangling from a horn
(*in Wright, 1998, 44*)

> In the falling snow
A laughing boy holds out his palms
> Until they are white
(in *Wright, 1998, 8*)

Both are vivid and joyful and resonate with meaning. Because Wright is Afro-

American, the second haiku is of particular interest because it can be interpreted as a child's play with snow. Is the boy experiencing the fulfilment of a desire to be white or is he feeling the sense of equality which comes when everyone, no matter their skin colour, is covered with snow?

By the early 1960s, other haiku translators, such as Geoffrey Bownas (1964) and Peter Beilenson (1962), joined the ranks of Blyth and Henderson. The result was that even more people grew aware of the haiku and eventually grass roots organizations, in the form of haiku study groups, began to flourish, especially in California (*Lamb 1979a*).

Haiku interest grew phenomenally in the '60s with the birth of the 'Hippy' culture and its interest in Eastern art, literature, music, religion and philosophy that far surpassed anything generated by the Beats. A major influence during this time was the philosopher Alan Watts whose writings and recordings used haiku (what he called the wordless poem) to illustrate Zen principles (*Higginson 1985, 67*). Thus, Watts reinforced the impression left by the Beats

that haiku had something to do with
Zen

In 1963, *American Haiku*, the first magazine devoted entirely to English-language
haiku, was published in Platteville,
Wisconsin *(Lamb 1979b)*. By the end of
the 1960s, the interest in haiku could no
longer be considered a fad. Haiku magazines and collections were being published on both coasts of the United
States as well as in the Canadian and
American Midwest.

In the 70s and 80s, the English-language
haiku became even more entrenched in
North American culture
with over a dozen periodicals at any one
time devoted to publishing the form as
well as its close relative, the senryu
(which was discussed in the chapter on
definition). Two of the longest-lived are
Frogpond, in its twenty-second year, currently edited by Jim Kacian, and *Modern
Haiku*, in its thirty first year and, for
practically all of this time, edited by
Robert Spiess, one of the seminal figures
in North American haiku.

Concomitant with the success of the
periodicals, has been the establishment of
various haiku societies. Three of them,
Haiku Society of America (founded in
1968 by H.G. Henderson and Leroy

Kanterman), Haiku Canada (established in 1977 by Eric Amann, Betty Drevniok and me)and Haiku Poets of Northern California (the origin of which is hazy but occurred somewhere in the late 1980s), have emerged as dominant, holding their own regular meetings and conferences as well as cooperating every two years to hold one major event, Haiku North America, that has attracted individuals from around the world. Each of the Societies also publishes a regular newsletter, with the Haiku Society of America also publishing its own journal, the already-mentioned *Frogpond*.

In the late 1980s, the renku and renga, both variations of linked haiku usually written in collaboration with others, have mushroomed in popularity with the result that about half of the haiku periodicals now publish one or two per issue. In fact, a couple of journals, *Air* and *Lynx,* were founded in the late eighties for the sole purpose of publishing such linked poems.

Why The Haiku Flourished in North America
Having established that the haiku has indeed flourished in North America, I

think an attempt should be made to explain why it became so strongly rooted in this part of the Western world. After all, French and British scholars and writers were the first to translate the form and to publish the first Western haiku. Should not, then, the haiku phenomenon have begun in one or both of these countries?

I have already given the two usual explanations: American enchantment with Japanese culture following World War II and the stamp of approval the influential Beats gave to the haiku. But what created this receptivity in the firstplace? The curiosity of the conqueror about the conquered? Guilt, both American and Canadian, about the internment of Japanese North Americans during World War II? Such explanations are worth exploring, but beyond the scope of this introduction.

Thomas Lynch (1989) has formulated another interpretation, one that has literary roots and therefore is directly relevant to this discussion. In his unpublished Ph.D.dissertation, he posits that an influential group of nineteenth-century New England poets, writers, and philosophers known as the

'Transcendentalists'created an intellectual and emotional climate receptive to the haiku. Lynch(1989, 3) argues that especially Walt Whitman, Henry David Thoreau and Ralph Waldo Emerson, developed a homegrown philosophy quite similar to Zen Buddhism and that this way of thinking permeated their writing which, in turn, strongly affected the work of important twentieth-century poets such as Ezra Pound, Wallace Stevens, William Carlos Williams, Richard Wright, Allen Ginsberg, and Gary Snyder. Not surprisingly, these names appear whenever haiku scholars, such as Higginson (1985), list the major poets who have written haiku or haiku-like poems.

Lynch's argument is compelling.In the work of Thoreau, the Transcendentalist most often cited as an influence by today's haiku poets, his concern with the immediate moment is clear:

In any weather, at any hour of the day or night, I have been anxious to improve the nick of time, and notch it on my stick too; to stand on the meeting of two eternities, the past and future, which is precisely the present moment; to toe that line[1889]1975, 179-180)

This attitude is very similar to those expressed by Whitman ([1892] 1969) and Emerson ([1840] 1971). Such Zen-like focus on the here-and-now is the sine qua non of haiku composition.

Lynch (1989, 58) goes so far as to speculate that a haiku-like poetry eventually would have evolved on its own in North America:

It seems to me possible, given the circumstances of American life and poetry, and given the direction established by Emerson, Thoreau, and Whitman, that a poetry very much like haiku, and perhaps even a philosophy very much like Zen, would have developed on this continent independently of any direct contact with Buddhism or Japanese literature.

Lynch has formulated an intriguing possibility, but whether these events would have transpired or not, is, in the final analysis, irrelevant. All that really matters, for the purposes of this discussion, is that an influential ideology predisposed North Americans to welcome the haiku because, at first glance, it seems to be a Zen-(or Transcendentalist-) based form of poetry.

What the practices of haiku reading and writing and Zen Buddhism certainly do have in common is that they both stress the importance of the present. Each approach argues that focusing on the immediate moment will result in illumination, or, what in Zen is called 'satori'and in haiku is referred to as a moment of awe or wonder.

This shared outlook is what attracted the Beats and Alan Watts. It is also what forms the heart of Lynch's hypothesis. But the haiku is, first and foremost, a form of poetry, not a vehicle for philosophical or religious expression.Study of the haiku's long history in Japan shows quite clearly that it has always been a form of poetry quite separate from Zen Buddhism. While the great Basho and a few other outstanding haiku poets were Zen monks, they all treated haiku as poetry first, and, if at all, as Zen second. It is well-known that Basho made his living by teaching students how to become masterful haiku poets, not how to be Zen monks. Zen instruction was the job of the monks on staff in the Zen monasteries. As eminent Japanese haiku scholar Harold G. Henderson confirms in his classic *An Introduction to Haiku* (1958, 21), "Only a comparatively few of Basho's poems are obviously religious."

In fact, Henderson (1958, 2-3) empha

sizes on numerous occasions that haiku is very much a form of poetry, such as when he states:

In the hands of a master a haiku can be the concentrated essence of pure poetry. Because the haiku is shorter than other forms of poetry it naturally has to depend for its effect on the power of suggestion, even more than they do.

Further evidence of the independence of haiku from Zen comes from another Japanese haiku scholar, Kenneth Yasuda. In his also classic book, *The Japanese Haiku* (1957), almost no mention is made of Zen as an influence.

Thomas Lynch has suggested a plausible reason why the haiku found such a hospitable environment in North America. Without question, this poetic style received immediate respectability because of its perceived link with Zen Buddhism, a philosophy which evoked in North Americans, particularly those with a literary bent, the influential nineteenth-century philosophy called Transcendentalism. It is ironic, then, that in the haiku's long Japanese history, Zen played a minor role.

With which viewpoint do most current haiku poets align themselves; Blyth's haiku as Zen medium or Henderson's haiku as pure poetry? My long study of the significant haiku periodicals, the major anthologies, the collections of influential haiku poets and the conferences and agendas of the various haiku societies suggests that Henderson's outlook is clearly the more popular, in keeping with the long-held prevailing view in Japan. A telling fact is that the Haiku Society of America's annual haiku contest, the longest-running and the most prestigious, is named after Henderson and not Blyth.

Nevertheless, the belief that Zen and haiku are inextricably intertwined continues to be held by a small, loosely-knit but active group of haiku poets. Its members feel the Zen practices enhance the composition and appreciation of haiku and some of them regularly meet at various Zen retreats found chiefly in the New England states. I wonder if the ghosts of the Transcendentalists can be found there as well.

Ironically, West-coast poet James W. Hackett (1968, 1983), the best-known and most influential advocate of haiku as expression of Zen, holds himself relatively aloof from this group as well as the general haiku movement. To the public at large, Hackett became the spokesper son for haiku after winning the first of a series of haiku contests run by Japan Air Lines. Lamb (1995, 10) describes the first, which was also the most successful: *In 1964 something over 41,000 haiku were submitted to their National Haiku Contest. Seventeen contests conducted by radio stations in different parts of the country screened the entries and five winners from each local contest were submitted for final judging by Alan Watts. Japan Air Lines published the 85 national entries in a booklet entitled Haiku '64. James W. Hackett won the grand prize of two round trip tickets to Japan.*

Note the date of the contest - 1964. This explains why it captured the public's attention in a way no subsequent contest did. As stated earlier, the sixties was the heyday for worship of things Japanese. By the way, the winning poem by Hackett is considered a masterpiece by the Zen-oriented as well as the regular haiku community:

A bitter morning:
Sparrows sitting together
Without any necks.
(*in Lamb 1995, 10*)

For three years (1981-83) I ran haiku workshops at Ryerson Polytechnic

University in Toronto and found that the majority of newcomers to haiku possessed an already established interest in Zen. They expected to heighten their Zen-ness by writing haiku.

In addition to having read some Hackett, many came to the first class imbued with Eric Amann's ([1969] 1978) *The Wordless Poem: A Study of Zen in Haiku,* essentially an essay self-published as a booklet. On page thirty-eight, Amann summarizes the view that these students found compelling:

The main point of this essay has been to show that haiku is not to be regarded primarily as a form of poetry, as is commonly assumed in the West, but as an expression of Zen in poetry, a living 'Way' similar to the 'Way of the Brush' and other manifestations of Zen in the arts and in literature.

Their dismay was palpable when I told them that the workshop was going to focus on haiku as poetry, not Zen. But it was nothing compared to the news that Eric Amann had by this time publicly (at Haiku Canada meetings) divorced himself from the idea of haiku as Zen and was embarrassed by the attention his old views still garnered.

In spite of this double-whammy, practically all students stayed with the workshops and became quite proficient at writing haiku as poetry (Swede 1981).

The Influence of the North-American Haiku Around the World

Once rooted, the vigorous North-American haiku spread its seeds through-out the English-speaking world and beyond. Subsequent growth has been especially rapid and widespread in the United Kingdom. One of the chief reasons for this fecundity was the influential Northumberland playwright, poet and publisher Peter Mortimer.

In the early 1980s he invited me to write an article on developments in North America for his literary magazine, IRON(which made its last appearance in 1997). This article, along with some of my haiku, appeared in 1984 (No. 44) and was followed in 1985 by two more issues (Nos. 45 & 46) containing haiku and commentary by British poets. Then, in 1992, Mortimer's IRON Press put out the tiny (three-by-four-inch), but hugely successful anthology *The Haiku Hundred* which contains work from the United Kingdom as well as elsewhere. Since then, IRON Press has also published several collections of haiku by British poets as well as an anthology of

work by members of the British Haiku
Society, *The Iron Book of British Haiku*
(1998) edited by David Cobb and Martin
Lucas.

Another reason for this sudden flowering was the 1990 founding of the British
Haiku Society (BHS) by poets James
Kirkup, Dee Evetts and David Cobb.
Run from both Essex and London, BHS
soon became a powerful force by holding monthly meetings, annual conferences as well as publishing its own journal, *Blithe Spirit*, currently edited by
Caroline Gourlay.

Around the same time as the founding of
BHS, a couple of independent haiku
periodicals also appeared - Brian
Tasker's *Bare Bones* (out of Somerset) and
Kevin Bailey's *The Haiku Quarterly* from
Wiltshire. Recently, two new publica-
tions have surfaced, *Presence* edited by
Martin Lucas in Lancaster and *Still* edit-
ed by ai li in London.

Similar progress has occurred in
Australia and New Zealand and, not sur-
prisingly, in countries speaking tongues
other than English, especially Holland,
Germany, Croatia and, most recently,
Russia, Poland, and Sweden.

Has Japan, where the haiku first blos-
somed, shown any interest in these

developments outside its shores? Most definitely. Currently, a number of Japanese literary periodicals, such as *Ko* and *The Plaza*, as well as more general publications, such as the newspapers *Mainichi Daily News* and *The Daily Yomiuri* and *The Asahi Evening News*, regularly publish English-language haiku. Several others, particularly *Poetry Nippon*, have had long commitments to the English haiku, but have ceased operations.

In 1989, the three major Japanese haiku societies, the Modern Haiku Association, the Association of Haiku Poets and the Association of Japanese Classical Haiku, formed theHaiku International Association. The purpose for the creation of this new umbrella organization was given in an official announcement mailed around the globe:

To promote friendship and mutual understanding among poets, scholars and others who share a common interest in haiku, though they may live in very distant parts of the world.

True to its stated aim, the Haiku International Association puts out its own periodical, *HI,* which publishes work from numerous countries in the original language and in Japanese.

About half of every issue, however, is devoted to haiku from Japan (which are printed in English as well as in Japanese). This makes sense considering that Japan still has far more Haiku poets than any other nation.

As we approach the twenty-first century, writers, teachers and scholars of haiku can justifiably argue that the form is the most popular poetry in the world. None of the other long-lived forms, such as the englyn, ghazal, limerick, rondeau, sapphics, sestina, sonnet and villanelle, are considered with such universal interest. This status is in no small way due to encouragement by the Japanese who, in addition to publishing work from everywhere, also hold international contests and conferences to which they invite, often with all expenses paid, the winners as well as the presenters.

Further proof of the haiku's widespread influence is that many notable Canadian and American poets use the form, or variations of it. A quick check of my bookshelves found haiku or haiku-like poems in the works of numerous Canadian and U.S. mainstream poets. Lynch's (1989) thesis about the legacy of the transcendentalists certainly offers one plausible explanation of why the haiku has had so much influence on poets from both sides of the border.

One more indicator of how the North American psyche has welcomed the haiku is the fact that the former Poet Laureate of the U.S. Robert Hass has 'championed haiku for many years' (*Welch 1995, 35*). An English professor at the University of California at Berkeley, Hass recently has published *The Essential Haiku: Versions of Basho, Buson, and Issa* (1994). The book is part of a series put out by New Jersey's *Ecco Press* called '*The Essential Poets*', and puts the three Japanese legends of haiku in the luminous company of poets such as Blake, Keats, Poe, Shakespeare and Whitman. It should not be long before the haiku gets the same attention in university curricula that it now enjoys at lower levels. A huge step in that direction was taken on July 12, 1996 when the American Haiku Archive was opened at the California State Library in Sacramento.

George Swede

Biographies _of_ _the_ _poets_

_ai_ _li_

was born in Malaya and was educated in Malaya,
France and England. She lives in London and is a
Property and Interiors consultant and a fellow of
The Royal Photographic Society. She is also pub-
lisher of the empty press and edits the interna-
tional quarterly, still, a journal of short verse.
She has published two books of haiku: _words by_
_ai li_ (1995) and _words 2 by ai li_ (1995).

Randy Brooks

directs the writing major at Millikin University,
Illinois, USA. He and his wife, Shirley Brooks,
have been co-editors and publishers of High/Coo
Press since 1976 and currently edit Mayfly a
haiku magazine. Brooks has received numerous
awards for haiku including the Haiku Society of
America's 1998 Henderson Award.
Recent publications include _School's Out: Selected_
Haiku of Randy Brooks Press Here, (Foster City,
CA), 1999 &_The Homestead Cedars_ The Virgil
Hutton Haiku Memorial Chapbook
Competition, (Normal, Illinois: Saki Press), 1999.

David _Burleigh_

was born in 1950, in the North of Ireland and
graduated from the University of Ulster in Social
Administration. He moved to Tokyo in 1978
where he is an associate professor at Ferris
University in Yokohama.Haiku collections ,
include _Winter Sunlight_ and _A Wandering Fly_. He
assisted Kato Koko with translations and in A
Hidden Pond: Anthology of Modern Haiku
(Kadokawa Shoten, 1997).

Margaret Chula

a New Englander by birth, graduated from Boston's Northeastern University in 1969, with a degree in English. From 1981 until 1992, she taught English and creative writing at in Kyoto's Doshisha Women's College and Kyoto Seika College. Her collections of haiku include *Grinding my ink* (1993), *This Moment* (1995), and *Haiga Cards* (1997), all by Katsura Press. She lives in Portland, Oregon.

David Cobb

was born in Harrow, Middlesex, England in 1926 and had a long and varied career as an educator. In 1990, he co-founded the British Haiku Society (with Dee Evetts) and in 1994 edited *The Genius of Haiku--Readings from R.H. Blyth*, published by the British Haiku Society, co-edited (with James Kirkup and Peter Mortimer) *The Haiku Hundred* (IRON Press, 1992) and (with Martin Lucas) *The Iron Book of British Haiku* (IRON Press, 1998). His haiku books, include *Jumping from Kiyomizu* (IRON Press, 1996) and three by Equinox Press:

Dee Evetts

was born in England in 1943, and has lived in New York City since 1990. A professional carpenter, he was a co-founder of the British Haiku Society in 1990. His first collection of haiku and longer poems, *A Small Ceremony,* was published in 1988. A second collection, *endgrain,* was published by Red Moon Press in 1997.

LeRoy Gorman

was born in 1949 and raised in Ontario. He is editor of the Haiku Canada Newsletter, and is noted for his visual haiku. Gorman's publications include: *Only Shadflies Have Come* (Swamp Press, 1979, *whose smile the ripple warps* (Underwhich Editions, 1980), *wind in the keys* (High/Coo Press, 1981), *heart's garden* (Guernica Editions, 1983), *glass bell* (King's Road Press, 1991).

Caroline Gourlay

was born in 1939 and brought up in Shropshire, England. Her life is divided between work in London and living with her husband, who farms on the Welsh Border. Three collections of her haiku have been published:*Reading All Night* (Hub Press 1999), *Through The Café Door* (Snapshot Press 1999) and *Crossing the Field* (Redlake Press, 1995). She is editor of Blithe Spirit, the journal of the British Haiku Society.

Lee Gurga

was born and raised in Chicago, but has spent most of his adult life as a dentist in the small Midwestern town of Lincoln, Illinois. His collections are: *a mouse pours out,* (High/Coo Press, 1988), *Fresh Scent: Selected Haiku of Lee Gurga,* (High/Coo Press, 1998), *In & Out of Fog,* (Press Here, 1997), *Nine Haiku,* (Swamp Press, 1997), *dogs barking,* (Lidia Press, 1996), and *The Measure of Emptiness,* (Press Here, 1991).

Penny Harter

was born in New York City in 1940 She currently teaches creative writing and literature at the Santa Fe Preparatory School. She has published 14 collections of poems, including five of haiku: *The Orange Balloon* (From Here Press, 1980), *From the Willow* (Wind Chimes Press,

1983), *In the Broken Curve* (Burnt Lake Press, 1984), *The Monkey's Face* (From Here Press, 1987), and *Shadow Play:* Night Haiku (Simon & Schuster, 1994).

Cicely Hill
was born in Cranbrook, Kent, England, on 20 December 1927. She attended Winchester County School and Winchester College of Art before marrying in 1953. She accompanied her husband, a British diplomat, to Tokyo where she lived for five years.She lives in West Sussex and has published one collection, *The Earth Drawn Inwards,* Waning Moon Press, 1997.

Gary Hotham
was born in Presque Isle, Maine, in 1950, and now lives in Gloucestershire, England.His ten haiku chapbooks include: *Pulling Out the Bent Nail* (Wind Chimes Press, 1988), *As Far as the Wind Goes* (Juniper Press, 1993), *The Wind's View* (Juniper Press, 1996), *Hairs & Hawk Circles* (tel-let Press, 1996), and *Breath Marks* (Canon Press 1999)

Jean Jorgensen
was born in a small two-room log cabin in Alberta, Canada in 1943. She completed a degree in nursing in 1966 and now resides in Edmonton, Alberta. Two collections of her haiku have been published by Four Seasons Corner Press: *New Kid on the Block* (1990) and *Border Crossing* (1993).

Dhugal Lindsay
was born in 1971 at Rockhampton, Queensland, Australia. As a double major in biochemistry and

Japanese studies at the University of Queensland, he became an exchange student in 1991 at Keio University, located in Japan In 1995 he earned an M.S. in aquatic biology from the University of Tokyo, where he is currently enrolled in the doctoral program. A collection of his haiku has not yet been published

Martin Lucas

was born in Middlesbrough, England in 1962, and earned an M.A. in religious studies from Lancaster University and a B.A. in English literature from the University of Kent at Canterbury. He is editor of *Presence*, a haiku periodical and is also co-editor (with David Cobb) of *The Iron Book of British Haiku* (IRON Press, 1998). His two haiku collections are: *darkness and light* (Hub Editions, 1996) and *bluegrey* (Hub Editions, 1994).

Peggy Lyles

was born in Summerville, South Carolina in 1939 and earned a B.A. from Columbia College and an M.A. in English at Tulane University in 1962. From 1980 until 1985 she was poetry editor of Georgia Journal. Lyle's first collection of haiku, *Red Leaves in the Air*, was published as a mini-chapbook by High/Coo Press in 1979. Her other two collections are *Still at the Edge* (Swamp Press, 1980) and *Prisms* (Wind Chimes Haiku Sheet, 1988).

Marlene Mountain

also known as Marlene Wills, was born in Ada, Oklahoma in 1939. A visual artist as well as poet, she currently paints and writes on a mountain in Hampton, Tennessee. Her first volume of haiku,

the old tin roof, was published in 1976. In the
1980s and 1990s Mountain focused on one-line
haiku, especially advocating political and femi-
nist perspectives. Her collection *equal, hell art*
(1982) includes what she calls 'haiku, untamed
haiku, beyond untamed haiku, & more'.

Bill Pauly

was born in 1942 in Davenport, Iowa .He is cur-
rently assistant professor of English at Loras
College, in Dubuque.Two collections of his
haiku have been published, *Wind the Clock by
Bittersweet* (High/Coo Press, 1977), and *Time
From His Bones* (Juniper Press 1978)

Raymond Roseliep

was born in 1917 in Farley, Iowa, and was
ordained for the priesthood at the Catholic
University of America in 1943. Book-length col-
lections of his haiku include *Listen to Light*
(Alembic Press, 1980), and *Rabbit in the Moo*n.
He has published fourteen chap books including
Sky in My Legs (Juniper Press, 1979), *Firefly in my
Eyecup* (High/Coo Press, 1979), and *The Earth
We Swing On* (Winston Press, 1984).

Alexis Rotella

was born in Johnstown, Penn. in 1947;in 1984
she was ordained as an interfaith minister. She
lives in Los Gatos, Ca. and has written more
than three dozen books and edited two haiku
anthologies, *Butterfly Breezes* (self-published in
1981) and *The Rise and Fall of Sparrows* (Los
Hombres Press, 1990). Collections include:
Rearranging Light (Muse Pie Press, 1985)*An
Unknown Weed* (King's Road Press, 1991).

George Swede

has published twenty-eight collections of poetry with about half involving solely haiku and related forms. He has also edited six anthologies in addition to *Global Haiku* and published about a dozen other books.Since 1968 he has worked at Ryerson Polytechnic University in Toronto where he is currently chair of the Department of Psychology and School of Justice Studies.Some recent publications include: *My Shadow Doing Something* (Tiny Poems Press 1997), and *Almost Unseen ; Selected Haiku of George Swede*(Brooks Books, 2000)

Vincent Tripi

was born in Brooklyn, New York in 1941. Since 1972 he has worked in various group-homes and residential treatment centers with children who are emotionally disturbed or physically abused. He now lives in Tempe, Arizona. His haiku publications include: *between God & the pine* (Swamp Press, 1997), *the path of the bird* (Hummingbird Press, 1996), *tribe: meditations of a haiku poet* (Swamp Press,1995), *white* (Swamp Press, 1994).

Makoto Ueda

is Professor Emeritus of Japanese at Stanford University and one of the world's foremost scholars of the haiku form. Two of his latest books are *Basho And His Interpreters: Selected Hokku with Commentary* (1991) and *The Path of Flowering Thorn: The Life and Poetry of Yosa Buson (*1998) both published by Stanford University Press.

Cor van den Heuvel

was born in Biddeford, Maine in 1931, and grew up in Maine and New Hampshire. He lives in New York city where he worked for *Newsweek* until his retirement in 1988. His Chant Press publications include: *Dark* (1982) and *Puddles* (1990), and Quebec's King's Road Press published *The Geese Have Gone in* 1992. He also edited *The Haiku Anthology,* first published by Doubleday in 1974, Simon & Schuster 1986 and Norton 1999.

Anita Virgil

was born in Baltimore, Maryland in 1931 and for several years was editorial assistant at *Town & Country* magazine. She lives in Forest, Virginia, has exhibited her paintings in numerous shows, and her three haiku collections include *One Potato Two Potato Etc* (1991) and *Pilot* (Peaks Press 1996)

Nick Virgilio

was born in 1928, in Camden, New Jersey. After graduating from Camden High School in 1946, he served with the Navy until 1948 and received a B.A. from Temple University in 1952. He had a successful career as an announcer and writer for radio, television and newspapers in the Camden area and, later in life, was Poet-in-Residence at the Walt Whitman International Poetry Centre. He died January 3, 1989. Burnt Lake Press published his *Selected Haiku* in 1985 and came out with a second edition in 1988.

Michael Dylan Welch

was born in 1962 in Watford, England. He is a staff editor with IDG Books Worldwide and lives in Foster City, California. From 1991-1997 he was editor of *Woodnotes*, the Haiku Poets of Northern California magazine.He is currently editor of a new magazine, *Tundra*, and continues to publish books under his own Press Here imprint, including *The Haijin's Tweed Coat* (1990).

Rod Willmot

was born in Toronto in 1948. In 1983 he founded Burnt Lake Press which was devoted to publishing the work of other haiku poets. He lives in Sherbrooke, Quebec. His first collection of haiku, *Haiku* (Editions Particuliéres), was published in 1969 followed by by *Sayings for the Invisible* (Black Moss Press, 1988). In 1983, he edited *Erotic Haiku* (Black Moss Press), and in 1985, published *The Ribs of Dragonfly* (Black Moss Press), the first book-length haibun in the English language.

Works Cited in The Text

Amann, E. (1978) *The Wordless Poem* (Revised ed.)
Toronto: The Haiku Society of America

Beilson, P. (1962) *Haiku Harvest.* Mount Vernon,
New York: The Peter Pauper Press

Blyth, R.H. [(1949) 1981] *Haiku* (4 vols) Tokyo:
Hokuseido Press

Bownas, G. and **Thwaite,** A. (1964) *The Penguin Book
of Japanese Verse.* Penguin Books Ltd., England

Brooks, R.M & **Gurga,** L.(1992) *Midwest Haiku
Anthology.* Decatur.IL:High/Coo Press

Bullock, A. & **Stallybrass,** O. (1977) *The Harper
Dictionary of Modern Thought.* New York: Harper &
Row

Buson.(1750?) About to bloom, in Raymond
Roseliep(1976).This haiku of ours in David Dayton
(ed.) (1980) *A Roseliep Retrospective.* Ithaca,New York:
Alembic Press

Cobb, D. (1997) *Spring Journey to the Saxon Shore.*
Shalford, Essex, UK: Equinox Press, 50

Emerson, R.W. (1840) The new poetry, in Perry
Miller (ed.) (1971) *The Trancendentalists.* Cambridge,
Mass.: (1972) Harvard University Press, 375-381

Ginsberg, A. (1978) *Mostly Sitting Haiku.* Paterson,
New Jersey: From Here Press

Ginsberg, A. (1977) I didn't know the names, in W.J.
Higginson (ed.)(1985) *The Haiku Handbook.* New
York: McGraw-Hill

Giroux, J. (1974) *The Haiku Form.* Rutland,VT:
Charles E. Tuttle

Gorman, L.(1979) a foot in George Swede (ed.)
Canadian Haiku Anthology. Toronto: Three Trees
Press, page 52

Gourlay, C. (1995) *Crossing the Field.* Clun,
Shropshire: The Redlake Press

Hackett, J.W. (1968) *Haiku Poetry* (4.Vols) Tokyo:
Japan Publications

Hackett, J.W. (1983) *The Zen Haiku and other Zen
poems of J.W. Hackett.* Tokyo: Japan Publications

Harter, P. (1987) *The Monkey's Face.* Fanwood, NJ:
From Here Press 8

Hass, R. (ed. trans.) (1994) *The Essential Haiku:
Versions of Basho, Buson & Issa.* Hopewell, New Jersey:
Echo Press

Henderson, H.G. (1934) *The Bamboo Room.* Boston:
Houghton Mifflin

Henderson, H.G. (1958) *An Introduction to Haiku.*
New York: Doubleday.

Henderson, H.G. (1967) *Haiku in English.* Rutland,
VT: Charles E. Tuttle

Higginson, W.J. (1982) Afro-American haiku.
Frogpond, Vol. 5, No. 2, 6

Higginson, W.J. (1985) *The Haiku Handbook.*
New York: McGraw-Hill

Higginson,W.J. (1996) *Haiku World.* Tokyo:Kodansha
International

Higginson, W.J. (1996) *The Haiku Seasons.*Tokyo:
Kodansha International

Hotham, G. (1998) *Pulling Out The Bent Nail.* Glen
Burnie, MD: Wind Chimes Press

Howard, D. and **Duhaime**, A. (eds) (1985) *Haiku
Anthology Canadienne/Canadian Anthology.* Hull, QC.
Les éditions Asticou

Kerouac, J. (1971) *Scattered Poems.* San Franciso: City
Lights Books, 74

Kirkup,J. **Cobb**, D. & **Mortimer**, P. (1992) *The Haiku
Hundred.* Cullercoats, North Shields, UK.: IRON
Press

Lamb, E.S. (1979a) A history of Western haiku (Part
1.) *Cicada,* Vol. 3, No. 1, 3-9

Lamb, E.S.(1979b) A history of Western haiku (Part 2)
Cicada, Vol. 3, No.2, 3-9

Lamb, E.S. (1995) Haiku in English to 1978, in *A
Haiku Path.* New York: Haiku Society of America
Inc., 3-21

Lynch, T.P. (1989) An original relation to the universe: Emersonian poetics of imminence and contemporary American haiku. unpublished Phd. University
of Oregon

Matsuo-Allard, R.C. (1977) Haiku: The original one-line poem. *Cicada*, Vol. 1 No. 4, 31-35

Mountain, M. (1986) 'one fly'. in C. van den Heuvel (ed) *The Haiku Anthology*, 1986.New York: Simon & Schuster

O' Brien, G. (1982) Charles Reznikoff: A difficult simplicity. *Frogpond*, Vol.5, No. 2, 20-22

Pope, A. (1739) I am his Highness' dog at Kew, in H.E. Richardson and F.B. **Shroyer** (eds) (1971) *Muse of Fire: Approaches to Poetry*. New York: A. Knopf, 238

Pratt, W. (1963) *The Imagist Poem*. New York: E.P.Dutton

Roseliep, R. (1979) On a rhyming planet. *Haiku Journal*, Vol.3, No.1, 31

Roseliep, R. (1980a) Time, in Bill Pauly (1980) A joyous dance in timeless, in David Dayton (ed) *A Roseliep Retrospective*. Ithaca, New York: Alembic Press, 46

Roseliep, R. (1980b) Spring breeze. *Cicada*,Vol. 4, No. 3, 6

Ross, B. (ed) (1993) *Haiku Moment: An Anthology of Contemporary North American Haiku*. Rutland VT: Charles E. Tuttle

Rotella, A. (1983) *On a White Bud*. Westfield, NJ: Merging Media

Stevens, W. (1971) *The Palm at the End of the Mind: Selected Poems and a Play*. edited by Holly Stevens. New York: Vintage Books

Swede, G. (ed) (1979) *Canadian Haiku Antholgy*. Toronto: Three Trees Press.

Swede, G. and **Amann**, E. (1980) Toward a definition of the modern English haiku. *Cicada*, Vol. 4, 3-12

Swede, G. (1981) *The Modern English Haiku*. Toronto: Columbine Editions

Swede, G. (1981) A haiku writing course. *Cicada*, Vol.5, No. 3. 3-6

Swede, G. (1984) The haiku redefined - again. *Poetry Canada Review*, Vol.5, No.3, 9

Swede, G. (1992) Elite Haiku: Hybrids of nature and human content. *Modern Haiku*, Vol. 23, No. 1, 65-72

Swede, G. (1996) *The North American Haiku: Empirical Studies establish defining criteria and future*

trends. Unpublished Ph.D , Greenwich University

Swede, G. (1999) Looking East: The haiku as a match for existing Western contexts - Some speculations and empirical evidence, a paper presented at Haiku North America 1999, Northwestern University, Evanston, IL July 8-11

Thoreau, H. D. (1889) *Henry David Thoreau: Essays, Journals and Poems* edited by Dean Flower (1975) Greenwich, Connecticutt: Fawcett

Ueda, M. (trans) (1976) *Modern Japanese Haiku: An Anthology*. Toronto: University Press

Ueda, M. (trans) (1991) *Basho and His Interpreters: Selected Hokku with Commentary*. Stanford, California: Stanford University Press.

Ungar, B. (1982) *Jack Kerouac as haiku poet*. Frogpond, Vol.5 , No.2, 12-19

van den Heuvel, C. (ed) (1974) *The Haiku Anthology*. New York: Anchor Press/Doubleday

van den Heuvel, C. (ed) (1986) *The Haiku Anthology*. New York: : Simon & Schuster

van den Heuvel, C. (1992) *The Geese Have Come*. Pointe Claire, QC: King's Road Press

van den Heuvel, C (1999) *The Haiku Anthology*. New York: W.W. Norton

Virgilio, N (1988) *Selected Haiku*. Windsor ON: Burnt Lake Press/Black Moss Press

Watts, A.W. (1960) *This Is It*. New York: Collier Books

Welch, M.D. (1995) Robert Hass named Poet Laureate of the United States. Woodnotes, No.25, 35

Whitman, W (1892) *Leaves of Grass*. Supplementary material by Francis Griffith (1969). New York: Avon Books

Williams, W.C. (1958) *I wanted to Write a Poem: The Autobiography of the Works of a Poet*. Reported and edited by Edith Heal. Boston: Beacon Press

Willmot, R (1980) *The woodcock's beak*. Cicada, Vol. 4, No. 3. 33-34

Wright, E. & **Fabre**, M. (1978) *Richard Wright Reader*. New York: Harper & Row

Wright, R. (1998) *Haiku:This Other World*. Edited by

Y. Hakatuni & R.L. Tenner. New York: Arcade
Publishing
Yasuda, K. (1957) *The Japanese Haiku*. Rutland, VT:
Charles E Tuttle
Yuasa, N. (trans) (1974) *Basho: The Narrow Road to
the Deep North and other Travel Sketches.*
Harmondsworth, England: Penguin Books

****

IRON HAIKU

*We are the UK's main independent haiku publisher. Try
some of our other titles. Add 50p per title for p & p. Our
address is on page two.*

The IRON Book of British Haiku.
Edited by David Cobb & Martin Lucas
£6.50. ISBN 0 906228 67 0
More than 70 writers, from the famous (Seamus) to
the unknown - the best haiku in recent years from
these shores.

The Dust is Golden
by Jackie Hardy
£4.00. ISBN 0 9806228 72 7
A beautiful miniature book where everyday objects,
feelings and moments are transmuted into something
extraordinary.

The Haiku Hundred
£3.50p. ISBN 0 906228 42 5
An even smaller page size (A7); one hundred haiku
from the 5, 500 submitted to this anthology. Like most
of our haiku books, it has been reprinted - four times.